Examining Issues Through Political Cartoons

Weapons of Mass Destruction

Edited by William Dudley

Bruce Glassman, *Vice President*
Bonnie Szumski, *Publisher*
Helen Cothran, *Managing Editor*
Scott Barbour, *Series Editor*

GREENHAVEN PRESS
An imprint of Thomson Gale, a part of The Thomson Corporation

THOMSON
GALE

Detroit • New York • San Francisco • San Diego • New Haven, Conn.
Waterville, Maine • London • Munich

For more information, contact
Greenhaven Press
27500 Drake Rd.
Farmington Hills, MI 48331-3535
Or you can visit our Internet site at http://www.gale.com

LIBRARY OF CONGRESS CATALOGING-IN-PUBLICATION DATA

Weapons of mass destruction / William Dudley, book editor.
   p. cm. — (Examining issues through political cartoons)
  Includes bibliographical references and index.
  ISBN 0-7377-1923-0 (lib. : alk. paper)
  1. Weapons of mass destruction. 2. World politics—1945-1989. 3. World politics—1989– 4. Weapons of mass destruction—Caricatures and cartoons.
5. World politics—Caricatures and cartoons. I. Dudley, William, 1964– II. Series.
  U793.W425 2005
  358'.3'0207—dc22
                                                    2004059689

Contents

Foreword

Political cartoons, also called editorial cartoons, are drawings that do what editorials do with words—express an opinion about a newsworthy event or person. They typically appear in the opinion pages of newspapers, sometimes in support of that day's written editorial, but more often making their own comment on the day's events. Political cartoons first gained widespread popularity in Great Britain and the United States in the 1800s when engravings and other drawings skewering political figures were fashionable in illustrated newspapers and comic magazines. By the beginning of the 1900s, editorial cartoons were an established feature of daily newspapers. Today, they can be found throughout the globe in newspapers, magazines, and online publications and the Internet.

Art Wood, both a cartoonist and a collector of cartoons, writes in his book *Great Cartoonists and Their Art*:

> Day in and day out the cartoonist mirrors history; he reduces complex facts into understandable and artistic terminology. He is a political commentator and at the same time an artist.

The distillation of ideas into images is what makes political cartoons a valuable resource for studying social and historical topics. Editorial cartoons have a point to express. Analyzing them involves determining both what the cartoon's point is and how it was made.

Sometimes, the point made by the cartoon may be one that the reader disagrees with, or considers offensive. Such cartoons expose readers to new ideas and thereby challenge them to analyze and question their own opinions and assumptions. In some extreme cases, cartoons provide vivid examples of the thoughts that lie behind heinous acts; for example, the cartoons created by the Nazis illustrate the anti-Semitism that led to the mass persecution of Jews.

Examining controversial ideas is but one way the study of political cartoons can enhance and develop critical thinking skills. Another aspect to cartoons is that they can use symbols to make their point quickly. For example, in a cartoon in *Euthanasia*, Chuck Asay depicts supporters of a legal "right to die" by assisted suicide as vultures. Vultures are birds that eat dead and dying animals and are often a symbol of repulsive and cowardly predators who take advantage of those who have met misfortune or are vulnerable. The reader can infer that Asay is expressing his opposition to physician-assisted suicide by suggesting that its supporters are just as loathsome as vultures. Asay thus makes his point through a quick symbolic association.

An important part of critical thinking is examining ideas and arguments in their historical context. Political cartoonists (reasonably) assume that the typical reader of a newspaper's editorial page already has a basic knowledge of current issues and newsworthy people. Understanding and appreciating political cartoons often requires such knowledge, as well as a familiarity with common icons and symbolic figures (such as Uncle Sam's representing the United States). The need for contextual information becomes especially apparent in historical cartoons. For example, although most people know who Adolf Hitler is, a lack of familiarity with other German political figures of the 1930s may create difficulty in fully understanding cartoons about Nazi Germany made in that era.

Providing such contextual information is one important way that Greenhaven's Examining Issues Through Political Cartoons series seeks to make this unique and revealing resource conveniently accessible to students. Each volume presents a representative and diverse collection of political cartoons focusing on a particular current or historical topic. An introductory essay provides a general overview of the subject matter. Each cartoon is then presented with accompanying information including facts about the cartoonist and information and commentary on the cartoon itself. Finally, each volume contains additional informational resources, including listings of books, articles, and websites; an index; and (for historical topics) a chronology of events. Taken together, the contents of each anthology constitute an amusing and informative resource for students of historical and social topics.

Introduction

War has been a constant of human history. As a result, the development of increasingly lethal weapons of war has been a constant as well. From sharp rocks to metal spears to the development of firearms and modern explosives and machine guns, humans have continued to create more and more powerful weapons to kill enemy soldiers and civilians and to destroy buildings and infrastructure. The twentieth century has witnessed the development and use of several types of weapons that are so devastating that they have been placed in a category of their own: weapons of mass destruction (WMD or WMDs). Such weapons are so destructive that the world's nations have taken steps to limit their use and possession; many countries have either forgone such weapons or have relinquished them. Weapons of mass destruction have been a recurring topic in national security debates in the United States, which has been at the forefront both of developing WMDs and of pursuing international disarmament.

While there have been some semantic disputes about which weapons should be classified as WMDs, most definitions encompass three main types: nuclear, chemical, and biological weapons. The three types of weapons work quite differently, but each has already been used to kill tens of thousands of people.

Nuclear Weapons

Nuclear weapons are perhaps the most feared of the WMDs. They are explosive devices that get their power from the transformation of matter into energy. They were first developed by the United States during World War II and were used by America against the Japanese cities of Hiroshima and Nagasaki in 1945. The virtually complete destruction of those cities, each by a single bomb, starkly illustrated the destructive capabilities of nuclear weapons to the world. Since 1945 several other nations have produced or acquired nuclear weapons, but they have not been used in war.

There are two main types of nuclear weapons. Fission weapons or atomic bombs, work through the fission (splitting) of atomic nuclei of the elements uranium or plutonium. When a neutron (a subatomic particle) strikes the nucleus of a uranium or plutonium atom, the atom splits, releasing a tremendous amount of energy and two or three other neutrons, which may then split other uranium nuclei to create a self-sustaining chain reaction and fission explosion. The bombs the United States dropped on Hiroshima and Nagasaki at the end of World War II were fission devices. Fusion, or thermonuclear, bombs actually use a fission bomb as a trigger —the fission blast creates extremely high temperatures that force the atomic nuclei of hydrogen atoms to combine. This fusion of atoms—the process by which the sun and stars get their energy— creates an even bigger explosion than fission bombs. The United States was the first nation to develop fusion weapons in 1952; some of the bombs it went on to make were the equivalent of hundreds of Hiroshima bombs.

Most people are familiar with the mushroom-shaped cloud created by a nuclear bomb explosion. The effects of a nuclear blast that creates these clouds are known both from the results of the World War II bombings as well as nuclear bomb tests conducted by the United States and other countries. They include both immediate blast effects as well as longer-lasting nuclear radiation. The blast created by the bomb dropped on Hiroshima was equivalent to about twelve thousand tons of the explosive TNT; it obliterated about five square miles of the city through a massive shock wave that created winds more powerful than a tornado, by an intense fireball of hot gas that vaporized everything it touched, and by an intense thermal radiation that ignited massive fires. An estimated eighty thousand Japanese immediately perished, either from effects of the blast or from skin burns (flash burns) caused by the intense heat radiation.

In addition to blast and fire effects, nuclear bombs creates deadly gamma rays and other radiation. Exposure to intense radiation can cause immediate sickness and death in humans, or cancer that may come years later. Besides the eighty thousand people in Hiroshima who perished immediately, another sixty thousand died by the end of 1945 due to radiation sickness. Those who received high radiation exposure and who survived were later found to have a greater risk of cancer years or decades later. Another danger of nuclear weapons is fallout—particles of material that have become radioactive and which are spread in the atmosphere before settling down to earth. These materials can travel around the world before descending with rain, snow, and fog. While most fallout dies off in a matter of hours or days, a few elements continue to give off radiation over a long period and may render areas uninhabitable.

Chemical Weapons

Chemical weapons use toxic chemical agents to kill or incapacitate people. They can take the form of gases, liquids, or powders. Modern chemical weapons were first used in World War I, when they were deployed by Germany, France, and Great Britain, and inflicted roughly ninety thousand fatalities and a million injuries.

Like nuclear weapons, chemical weapons can be classified into various subtypes. Blister agents are chemicals that cause blisters on the skin and create respiratory damage and blindness. The most commonly used blister agent is mustard gas. Choking agents are heavier gases such as chlorine and phosgene that create fluid buildup in the lungs and cause people to die from lack of oxygen. Blood agents such as hydrogen cyanide work by preventing the blood from utilizing oxygen. Germany, France, and Great Britian used all of these types of weapons in World War I . Of the "classic" chemical weapons mustard gas remains the most popular to this day because of its relative ease and low cost of production and its capacity to inflict injuries. Mustard gas was used by Iraq in its 1980–1988 war against Iran.

In the 1930s scientists in Germany discovered a new class of chemical weapons called nerve agents. These were much more lethal than World War I–era weapons and could enter the body both through inhalation and through the skin. They work by blocking the flow of acetylcholinestrase, an enzyme crucial to the functioning of the nervous system, causing loss of muscle control and death. Nerve agents, including sarin and VX, were a central part of chemical weapons research by the United States and other nations after World War II.

Biological Weapons

Biological weapons contain germs or other live agents that have been developed for use as weapons against humans, livestock, and crops; they can kill or incapacitate their targets either through poisoning or disease. They include bacteria (cholera, the plague), viruses (smallpox, encephalitis), and certain toxins produced by plants and other organisms, such as ricin (derived from castor beans).

Biological weapons are unique in that they can vary greatly in their incubation time—the period between when the agent infects and when disease symptoms first appear. They are also unique in that they can reproduce; thus a small biological weapons attack can potentially cause mass casualties as the living agents reproduce and spread among a population. Biological weapons have not been used often in war since the beginning of the twentieth century. Perhaps the most notorious example of their use was when Japan used germs against China in the 1930s, killing hundreds of thousands of people.

Problems of WMDs

Obviously, there are many differences between nuclear, chemical, and biological weapons. However, they share similarities that have caused them to be lumped together as WMDs. One important characteristic they share is that they can be used indiscriminately against mass numbers of people, making no distinction between soldiers and civilians. Critics have judged the use of such weapons especially immoral for this reason.

The indiscriminate nature of many WMDs creates practical as well as ethical problems in their use. For example, armies releasing poisonous gases during World War I sometimes ran afoul of shifting winds that turned the poisonous gases back on them. Infectious biological agents can also end up harming those who launch them. Japan used some biological weapons against China in the 1930s, but stopped after its efforts to spread cholera, the plague, and other diseases resulted in hundreds of deaths of Japan's own troops. Nuclear weapons may also harm the attackers as well as their target. A nuclear attack creates radioactive fallout that can spread around the globe. In addition, many experts theorize that nuclear explosions could cause massive weather changes and global environmental damage that would render any "victory" achieved moot.

While critics of WMDs decry their indiscriminate destructiveness, some defenders respond by arguing that such weapons are valuable even if they are not actually used in wartime. Countries can use the threat of using WMDs to deter other nations from aggressive warfare—including using their own WMDs. Thus the United States and other nations persisted in developing biological and chemical weapons after World War I, but did not use such weapons during World War II. Historians ascribe the absence of chemical weapons attacks in World War II to nations unwilling to risk retaliation in kind.

Deterrence also played a significant role in the long Cold War (1946–1991) between the United States and the Soviet Union when the two adversaries raced to develop larger and more sophisticated arsenals of nuclear weapons. By the late 1950s both superpowers had enough bombs to destroy each other many times over. While tensions between the two countries remained high, war did not break out between them because leaders of both nations were unwilling to risk the nuclear destruction of their homeland that might result from an attack. Theorists later codified this idea as the mutual assured destruction (MAD) theory. The MAD theory depended on the existence of nuclear weapons and a stated willingness by the two adversaries to use them in self-defense. Many unnerved people, in pondering the paradox of threatening to use nuclear weapons to avoid nuclear war, believed that MAD lived up to its acronym. But, paradoxical or not, and despite some close calls, the Soviet Union and the United States did manage to avoid nuclear war; some observers have argued that a similar nuclear "balance of terror" has prevented additional wars between rivals India and Pakistan since both nations developed their own nuclear arsenals.

WMDs can create problems for the people and nations that make them regardless of whether they are used in war. Nuclear testing in the United States in the 1950s and 1960s created radioactive fallout that, according to some estimates, is to blame for seventeen thousand cancer deaths. (The United States and Soviet Union negotiated a ban on aboveground nuclear tests in 1963.) Millions of people in Kazakhstan who lived upwind of Soviet nuclear tests have suffered from cancer, birth defects, and weakened immune systems. In the Russian town of Sverdiovsk in 1979, more than sixty people died when a bioweapons plant accidentally released anthrax spores and caused an outbreak of inhalational anthrax. The creation, stabilization, storage, transportation, and disposal of chemical weapons have also created significant environmental problems in the countries that have had chemical weapons programs. Russia has hundreds of formerly secret chemical weapons dumps that are leaking poisons into the water and soil. The United States is not immune from such problems; in one 1969 incident in Utah, the accidental release of poison gas killed thousands of sheep and left residents facing long-term health problems.

International Efforts to Control WMDs

Because weapons of mass destruction raise such severe moral and practical problems, they have been a longtime focus of international treaties and agreements that seek to control their possession, development, and use. Following the gas horrors of World War I, nations agreed in the 1925 Geneva Protocol to ban "the use in war of asphyxiating, poisonous or other gases, and of bacteriological methods of warfare." However, the protocol did not ban the manufacture and stockpiling of these weapons. In 1963, after five years of negotiations, the United States, the Soviet Union, and Great Britain agreed to a ban of nuclear tests in the atmosphere, underwater, and in space. The 1968 Nuclear Nonproliferation Treaty (NPT), created and signed by sixty-two nations in 1968, committed signatory nations to refrain from developing nuclear weapons if they had not already done so, and for existing nuclear powers to refrain from spreading nuclear technology (the number of signatory nations has since grown to 187). The 1972 Biological and Toxin Weapons Convention, a UN treaty that forbids that production and stockpiling of such weapons, was signed by more than one hundred nations at its inception, though some countries, notably the Soviet Union, maintained their biological weapons programs in violation of the treaty's provisions. The 1993 Chemical Weapons Convention, which has been signed by more than 140 nations, bans the production and possession of chemical weapons and commits nations to eventually destroy their stockpiles. These are but a fraction of the multilateral and bilateral treaties that have been created to control WMDs. Whether these treaties can be adequately enforced and whether nations can be entrusted to live up to their commitments has been a matter of constant debate.

WMDs and Terrorism

The twenty-first century may differ from the twentieth, many predict, by the declining importance of conflict between states and the growth of conflict involving nonstate actors, especially transnational terrorist groups. The rising concern with terrorism has reshaped the public debate over weapons of mass destruction and how nations should deal with them. Terrorist groups are not participants or signatories to international treaties and are not bound by the laws governing relations between countries. Many terrorists have also used suicidal tactics—which suggests to many that the traditional forms of deterrence that have prevented WMD use by nation-states may not work with terrorists.

An attack by terrorists using a weapon of mass destruction is not unprecedented; on March 20, 1995, members of Aum Shinrikyo, an extremist religious cult, released sarin gas in the Tokyo subway system. The attack, which involved five bags of the nerve agent, killed twelve commuters and injured more than five thousand. Some experts point to this and other recent terrorist events as evidence of a "new breed" of terrorists willing to inflict mass casualties. While in the past terrorist and insurgent groups with negotiable political demands may have considered WMDs as being ultimately damaging to their political cause, this new breed of terrorist may not, writes terrorism expert Walter Laqueur: "The state of affairs is different with regard to terrorists of the lunatic fringe, certain religious fanatics, and terrorist groups that are not interested in negotiations, but want to destroy the enemy."

The September 11, 2001, terrorist attacks did not involve nuclear, biological, or chemical weapons, but the horrific violence left many Americans wondering what would have happened if the perpetrators had them. Osama bin Laden, the leader of the al Qaeda terrorist network and alleged mastermind of the September 11 attacks has been quoted as saying that "we [al Qaeda] don't consider it a crime if we tried to have nuclear, chemical, biological weapons" in his declared holy war against the United States. For many Americans, the prospect of a nuclear attack by America's Cold War enemy, the Soviet Union, has been replaced by the nightmare possibility of a terrorist attack involving biological, chemical, or even nuclear weapons.

The Debate Continues

For more than a century the United States and the world have grappled with the problem of how to deal with chemical, biological, and nuclear weapons. Debates have raged over how to respond to enemies with such weapons, as well as whether the United States itself should possess and use WMDs. These debates are reflected in the work of political cartoonists, many of whom, such as Herbert L. Block of the *Washington Post*, have made WMDs personified characters in their work. The work in this volume provides a sampling of the commentary of political cartoonists about historical and current debates over WMDs, the efficacy of international treaties, and the question of whether such weapons are evil in and of themselves—or only if they fall in the wrong hands.

Chapter 1

The Atomic Bomb: A New Doomsday Weapon

Preface

The first—and thus far only—use of a nuclear weapon of mass destruction was America's dropping of two atomic bombs on Japan. President Harry S. Truman's decision to use the bombs not only hastened the surrender of the Japanese and the end of World War II, but opened the world's eyes to the awesome power of the weapons.

Truman had been president of the United States for less than two weeks (the vice president had become president after Franklin D. Roosevelt's death) when on April 25, 1945, Secretary of War Henry L. Stimson delivered a report to him that began: "Within four months, we shall in all probability have completed the most terrible weapon ever known in human history." That weapon was the atomic bomb—a weapon that got its enormous destructive power from splitting atoms and turning matter into energy. It had been developed in a massive secret wartime effort called the Manhattan Project, undertaken in part because of fears that Nazi Germany was working to develop its own bomb. The first atomic bomb was successfully tested in New Mexico in July 1945.

By then, Truman was meeting with the leaders of the Soviet Union and Great Britain in Potsdam, Germany, to discuss postwar plans. World War II was almost—but not quite—over. Germany had surrendered unconditionally on May 8, 1945 (fears that Germany might develop the atomic bomb helped spur the Manhattan Project). The United States had been successfully advancing against Japanese forces in the Pacific and was planning an invasion of the Japanese mainland—an operation that undoubtedly would have resulted in thousands, perhaps hundreds of thousands, of casualities. After America and its allies issued an ultimatum for Japan to surrender,

Truman returned from Potsdam and, in consultation with both military and civilian advisers, made the decision to use the new weapon against Japan.

On August 6, 1945, a U.S. plane dropped an atomic bomb on the Japanese city of Hiroshima. The explosion—the equivalent of twelve thousand tons of TNT—destroyed five square miles of the city and killed between seventy thousand and one hundred thousand people. Soon after the Hiroshima bombing, President Truman issued a statement that for most people was the first they had heard of the new weapon:

> Sixteen hours ago an American airplane dropped one bomb on Hiroshima. . . . It is an atomic bomb. It is a harnessing of the basic power of the universe. The force of from which the sun draws its power has been loosed against those who brought war to the Far East. . . . We are now prepared to obliterate more rapidly and completely every productive enterprise the Japanese have above ground in any city. . . . If they do not now accept our terms [of surrender] they may expect a rain of ruin from the air, the like of which has never been seen on this earth.

Two days later, the Soviet Union declared war on Japan. On August 9, a second atomic bomb was dropped on Nagasaki, leaving another seventy-five thousand Japanese dead or wounded. Many would die later from radiation poisoning. The bombs were a major factor in Japan's decision to surrender.

In his initial statement after Hiroshima, Truman also made a promise about the future:

> The fact that we can release atomic energy ushers in a new era in man's understanding of nature's forces. . . . I shall . . . make . . . recommendations to the Congress as to how atomic power can become a powerful and forceful influence towards the maintenance of world peace.

The president recognized that America and the world had entered a new era—one in which a future global conflict could have even more devastating consequences than the carnage of World War I and World War II. The joy most Americans felt at the victorious end of World War II was tempered to some extent by worries over what might happen if a World War III ever occurred. Joy over victory was also tempered, at least in the minds of some Americans, by guilt over the fact that the United States became the first (and thus far the only) nation to use such a weapon in war—one that indiscriminately killed so many Japanese civilians. To the end of his life Truman defended against critics his decision to use the atomic bomb; historians continue to debate the question today.

Examining Cartoon 1:
"For Whom the Bell Tolls"

About the Cartoon

The United States developed the atomic bomb in secret during World War II. On August 6 and 9, 1945, America dropped two atomic weapons on the Japanese cities of Hiroshima and Nagasaki, demolishing both cities and killing tens of thousands of citizens. Meanwhile, on August 8, the Soviet Union officially declared war on Japan and began moving troops into Manchuria, a Chinese province then occupied by Japan.

The initial reaction of many Americans to these events was excitement over the possibility that the war would soon be over. The cartoon by Fred O. Seibel, published on August 10, 1945, expresses the view that the final bell was tolling for Japan even if the country's leadership tried not to hear it. On August 14, Japan agreed to end the war. Despite the massive devastation caused by the bombs, many commentators supported their use as a means to end the war and avoid an American invasion of the Japanese mainland.

About the Cartoonist

Fred O. Seibel began his political cartoonist career in 1916 for the *Knickerbocker Press* in Albany, New York. From 1926 to 1968 he was the editorial cartoonist for the *Richmond Times-Dispatch*, where he gained national recognition for his work. A trademark of his cartoons was "Moses Crow," a recurring character who appeared in and sometimes commented on his cartoons (he can be seen in the lower left corner of this cartoon).

Examining Cartoon 2:
"Baby Play with Nice Ball?"

'BABY PLAY WITH NICE BALL?'

About the Cartoon

The above cartoon by famed British cartoonist David Low first appeared in the *London Evening Standard* on August 9, 1945, when news had arrived that America had dropped an atomic bomb on the Japanese city of Nagasaki—three days after the first atomic bomb was dropped on Hiroshima. The cartoon shows a scientist offering a ball representing atomic power to an infant representing humanity; the cartoon suggests that humanity might not be mature enough to handle the incredible powers scientists had discovered in unleashing atomic energy. In notes written for the cartoon compilation *Years of Wrath*, published in 1946, Low wrote about the cartoon: "The news of the appalling destruction at Hiroshima and Nagasaki was followed by the revelation that . . . British and American scientists had succeeded in solving the problems of nuclear fission and the release of atomic energy. Thus victory brought a question of crucial importance to the human race: Would Man, so ingenious in invention, apply the new discovery to the constructive arts of peace . . . ? Or would he . . . use it as yet another means to the conquest of power, thereby risking his own utter destruction?"

About the Cartoonist

David Low, a native of New Zealand, moved to Great Britain in 1919 and became one of that country's foremost political cartoonists and caricaturists. He worked for many years for the *London Evening Standard*.

Low. *London Evening Standard*, 1945.

Examining Cartoon 3:
"Eventually, Why Not Now?"

About the Cartoon

This cartoon by Jay Norwood "Ding" Darling, first published shortly after the United States dropped two atomic bombs on Japan in August 1945, reacts to the news by speculating what might happen if such weapons were used in a future war. It shows the planet's sole survivor trying to see if there is anyone left with whom to start a world organization to outlaw war. The irony of the cartoon stems from the fact that the world has been destroyed and the "survivor" is a charred corpse. The cartoon suggests that humanity must create a world peace organization before it is too late. Although the League of Nations, created after World War I, had failed to prevent the next world war, the United States did help establish another such organization even as it was fighting World War II: The United Nations was officially founded on October 24, 1945.

About the Cartoonist

Jay Norwood Darling, who signed his cartoons as "Ding," drew more than seventeen thousand cartoons for the *Des Moines Register* during a long career that spanned 1906 to 1949. Beginning in 1917, his work was also published in the *New York Tribune* and nationally syndicated, making Darling one of the nation's foremost cartoonists of his time. Darling received the Pulitzer Prize for cartoons in 1924 and 1943. His career spanned both the creation of the League of Nations after World War I and the United Nations after World War II—institutions he strongly supported.

Chapter 2

The Evolving Nuclear Threat

EXAMINING ISSUES THROUGH
POLITICAL CARTOONS

Preface

For four years beginning in 1945, the United States of America held a monopoly on nuclear weapons. That changed abruptly in August 1949 when the Soviet Union successfully tested an atomic bomb. By then relations between the two World War II allies had worsened over the fate of central Europe and other issues, beginning a long period of intense rivalry and mutual distrust between the two powers that became known as the Cold War.

The history of nuclear weapons in large part reflects the history of the Cold War, which lasted from the late 1940s until the Soviet Union's dissolution in 1991. During this time the United States and the Soviet Union built and deployed most of the world's arsenal of nuclear weapons. In 1952 the United States successfully exploded a hydrogen, or thermonuclear, bomb—a bomb that gets its energy from fusing atomic nuclei rather than splitting them, and which is hundreds of times more powerful than the bombs dropped on Japan. The Soviet Union tested its own hydrogen device in 1955. The Soviets developed the first submarines equipped with nuclear missiles in the 1950s and launched the first land-based intercontinental ballistic missile (ICBM) in 1957. The United States, having previously relied on aircraft as its nuclear delivery system, developed its own submarine and land-based missiles in 1959. By then a rough "balance of terror" had been achieved; both superpowers possessed the capability to inflict massive damage on each other in the event of actual fighting. Theorists dubbed the situation between the two superpowers mutually assured destruction, or MAD, because any attack by one side would result in large-scale destruction for both sides. At this point nuclear weapons became a deterrent against attack; they were necessary to possess, but were never to be actually used.

Nuclear war almost broke out during the 1962 Cuban missile crisis, when America confronted the Soviet Union over missiles deployed in Cuba. The crisis was averted when the Soviet Union agreed to remove the missiles; the following year the United States and the Soviet Union (along with Great Britain) approved a treaty to stop the aboveground testing of nuclear weapons. The United States and Soviet Union subsequently negotiated several other arms control treaties while continuing to develop and modernize their nuclear arsenals. Within the United States there was much debate over whether nuclear arms treaties were worthwhile and whether the Soviet Union should be trusted to adhere to them.

A few other nations also sought to join the "nuclear club" during and after the Cold War. Great Britain exploded its first atomic device in 1945, France joined the club in 1960, and China developed its first bomb in 1964. In 1968 the United Nations approved a Nuclear Nonproliferation Treaty; signatory nations pledged not to develop nuclear weapons or (if they already had them) to help other nations obtain them. The bulk of the world's nuclear arsenal, however, remained in the hands of the Soviet Union and the United States.

The bipolar nuclear standoff between the Cold War superpowers changed greatly in the late 1980s and early 1990s. A new Soviet president, Mikhail Gorbachev, sought to bring changes to the Soviet system and U.S.-Soviet relations. The result was a series of far-reaching arms control treaties and unilateral actions by both countries to reduce their nuclear arsenals. The breakup of the Soviet Union into Russia and several other countries in 1991 put a formal end to the Cold War. In 1996 the Ukraine, Belarus, and Kazakhstan transferred their nuclear weapons to Russia. Both Russia and the United States took steps to "stand down" the nuclear missiles pointed at each other in the 1990s.

For Americans, the nuclear nightmare of an all-out nuclear war between the United States and the Soviet Union was replaced by a new nightmare scenario—an attack on America with nuclear weapons carried out by other countries, or even terrorist groups. Since the end of the Cold War such nations as Pakistan, North Korea, Iraq, and Iran have pursued nuclear weapons with varying degrees of success. Foreign policy experts have debated whether the MAD idea of nuclear deterrence, which successfully prevented nuclear war during the Cold War, would have an effect on rogue nations or terrorist groups. They argue that deterrence would not necessarily work on terrorists who use suicide bombing tactics with car bombs and other conventional explosives, including, notably, the terrorists who instigated the September 11, 2001, attacks on America. Nuclear weapons of mass destruction have thus remained a serious American foreign policy concern even after the Cold War.

Examining Cartoon 1:
"Peace Today"

About the Cartoon

This cartoon by Reuben Goldberg was published in the *New York Sun* on July 22, 1947, a time when the United States had a monopoly on atomic weapons. It depicts a representative American family and its house resting on a large atomic bomb teetering on the edge of a cliff. The cartoon visually makes the argument that the world must either place these new weapons under world control or face world destruction. The United States did present a plan to the United Nations placing atomic weapons and materials under control of an international body, but the plan was rejected by the Soviet Union, which by then was working on developing its own atomic bomb. This cartoon won Goldberg the 1948 Pulitzer Prize.

About the Cartoonist

Reuben (Rube) Goldberg attained fame and fortune as a comic strip artist and cartoonist in the early twentieth century; he is perhaps most famous for his recurring cartoons of "Rube Goldberg Inventions"—outlandishly complicated machines for performing simple tasks. He became a political cartoonist relatively late in life, joining the staff of the *New York Sun* in 1938 when he was fifty-five. He worked at the *Sun*, often in collaboration with cartoonist Warren King, until 1950, then continued as editorial cartoonist for the *New York Journal* until he retired in 1964.

Goldberg. *New York Sun*, 1947.

Examining Cartoon 2:
"Let Me Know When You Decide Something"

About the Cartoon

In September 1949, America's monopoly on nuclear weapons ended when the Soviet Union exploded its own device. The shocking news resulted in a nuclear arms race between the two world superpowers. In January 1950 President Harry S. Truman ordered an accelerated development of a thermonuclear (hydrogen) bomb. America exploded its first such bomb—a device that was hundreds of times more powerful than the fission bombs dropped on Japan—on November 1, 1952. The Soviets exploded a thermonuclear bomb ten months later; over the next few years both sides set off dozens of such bombs to test and improve their effectiveness. Meanwhile, a UN Disarmament Commission was formed in 1953; representatives from the United States, Soviet Union, France, Canada, and Great Britain met periodically for talks about a nuclear test ban and other disarmament issues.

This cartoon by *Washington Post* cartoonist Herbert Block first appeared on April 24, 1957. It shows arms negotiators working in the shadow of "Mr. Atom," a menacing personification of "the bomb" that made numerous appearances in Block's cartoons. Block's character served as a recurring reminder of the threat of nuclear annihilation that overshadowed the world. While "Mr. Atom" appears relaxed, Block suggests in this cartoon that the international community should view nuclear disarmament talks with a greater sense of urgency.

About the Cartoonist

Herbert Block, better known by his pseudonym "Herblock," was a multiaward-winning editorial cartoonist who worked for the *Washington Post* newspaper from 1945 until his death in 2001.

Examining Cartoon 3:
"On-Site Inspection"

"IF WE EVER DECIDE TO GIVE THE AMERICANS ON-SITE INSPECTION OF THESE MISSILES THE SITES WILL BE WASHINGTON, NEW YORK, CHICAGO, LOS ANGELES ... "

About the Cartoon
Through the 1960s, 1970s, and 1980s, the Soviet Union and the United States continued to build and develop their nuclear arsenals, including missiles capable of delivering nuclear bombs to their targets in less than an hour. At the same time the two countries continued diplomatic talks aimed at limiting or reducing nuclear arsenals. The Strategic Arms Limitation Talks (SALT) in the late 1960s and 1970s resulted in several agreements to limit the construction of intercontinental and antiballistic missiles. In 1982 the United States and Soviet Union began a new series of negotiations called START (Strategic Arms Reduction Talks), with the United States calling for deep cuts in land-based missiles.

A recurring stumbling block over arms treaties was how they could be verified. American negotiators often proposed on-site inspections. The Soviet Union consistently objected to such conditions as a violation of its sovereignty. American critics of arms control efforts often argued that the Soviet refusal to permit on-site inspections indicated that the Soviets were likely to violate arms control treaties, leaving America behind in the arms race—and perhaps vulnerable to a Soviet nuclear first strike. This cartoon expounds this view. It shows two smug Soviet generals saying the only way they will let Americans have on-site inspections of their nuclear weapons is by "delivering" them to American cities. According to the cartoonist, the main threat facing America is not nuclear weapons themselves, but weapons in the hands of its Cold War enemy.

About the Cartoonist

Wayne Stayskal is the editorial cartoonist for the *Tampa Tribune*. His work has been collected in several books including *Liberals for Lunch*.

Examining Cartoon 4:
"What's Scarier?"

About the Cartoon

By the end of the twentieth century, the Soviet-American Cold War framework that had dominated the nuclear weapons issue went through a drastic turnaround. In the 1980s a new Soviet leader, Mikhail Gorbachev, introduced major internal reforms and diplomatic changes, including a willingness to let Eastern Europe break free from Soviet control. An attempted military coup by Communist hardliners in 1991 failed; by the end of the year the Soviet Union had dissolved into Russia and fourteen smaller countries. Relations between the United States and Russia improved as the Cold War came to an end.

These dramatic changes resulted in significant progress in arms control talks. In 1987 U.S. president Ronald Reagan and Gorbachev signed a treaty calling for the destruction of all intermediate-range nuclear missiles in Europe and the western Soviet Union. The Strategic Arms Reduction Treaty (START I), signed in 1991, called for a mutual reduction of strategic nuclear arsenals by about 25 percent. In 2002, U.S. president George W. Bush and Russian president Vladimir Putin signed an arms reduction agreement that called for the countries to deactivate 75 percent of their strategic nuclear arsenals.

Some critics of the 2002 treaty believed that Russian and American nuclear warheads should not be simply deactivated and placed in storage, but destroyed. One reason given was the possibility that other nations or terrorist groups might obtain access to nuclear weapons—a possibility suggested in this cartoon. Cartoonist Steve Breen compares the Cold War scenario of Russian missiles aimed at U.S. cities with the newer scenario of "deactivated" Russian weapons being rather loosely guarded. The Soviet Union and the United States had, after all, refrained from actually using nuclear weapons during the four decades of the Cold War. Whether terrorists might obtain and use nuclear weapons over the next forty years remains to be seen.

About the Cartoonist

Steve Breen became the staff political cartoonist for the *San Diego Union-Tribune* in 2001, having previously held the same position for the *Asbury Park Press* in New Jersey. He won the Pulitzer Prize for political cartoons in 1998.

Examining Cartoon 5:

"Oh, Yeah? Well, Now We, Too, Are a Great Power!"

About the Cartoon

India and Pakistan have a history of conflict, having fought three wars—in 1948, 1965, and 1971. The tensions between the two nations is especially alarming because both countries possess nuclear weapons. In 1974 India exploded an atomic bomb, and in 1998 both India and Pakistan conducted a series of nuclear tests that raised alarms around the world.

The above cartoon shows one reaction to the nuclear standoff between India and Pakistan. It depicts a Pakistani and an Indian, both with atomic bombs in tow. The Pakistani is asserting that his country is now a great power on par with India. The people's tattered clothes and primitive carts suggest that neither country has attained the economic, social, and technological development that is the mark of a great power and that each side's claim to greatness is therefore a hollow boast. The cartoon can also be interpreted as attributing the motive for India and Pakistan to build such weapons to petty national rivalry.

About the Cartoonist

John Trever is editorial cartoonist for the *Albuquerque Journal*. His work has been collected in several books including *Trever's First Strike* and *The Trever Gallery: A Public Hanging*.

Examining Cartoon 6:

"How Dare You Have a Nuclear Weapons Program!"

About the Cartoon

One of the leading countries of concern for people worried about nuclear proliferation is North Korea, a small and impoverished Communist country in Asia. North Korea shocked the world in 2002 when it confirmed it possessed a uranium enrichment program for making nuclear weapons. This program was in violation of the Nuclear Nonproliferation Treaty, which North Korea signed in 1985. It also placed into jeopardy the "Agreed Framework" developed between the United States and North Korea in 1994, in which North Korea pledged to freeze and eventually dismantle its plutonium-based nuclear weapons program in exchange for economic and energy assistance from the United States. In April 2003 North Korea's leaders told U.S. officials they possessed nuclear weapons, and in October of that year said they were extracting plutonium from spent fuel rods to produce nuclear weapons, an open violation of the Agreed Framework.

The United States condemned North Korea's actions and sought to enlist other nations to join in diplomatic talks to discuss an agreement to end North Korea's nuclear weapons program. However, some have criticized the Nuclear Nonproliferation Treaty and other international efforts to prevent the spread of nuclear weapons. They claim these attempts are a means by which the United States and other members of the "nuclear club" prevent other nations from becoming nuclear powers. This cartoon suggests that the United States is being hypocritical in demanding that North Korea dismantle what is a very small weapons program, at least compared to that of the United States.

About the Cartoonist

Steve Benson, a longtime staff cartoonist for the *Arizona Republic*, won a Pulitzer Prize for his work in 1993.

Chapter 3

Chemical and Biological Weapons

EXAMINING ISSUES THROUGH
POLITICAL CARTOONS

Preface

In addition to nuclear weapons, chemical and biological weapons have also been classified as weapons of mass destruction. Chemical weapons are poisonous chemical materials that kill or incapacitate the enemy. Biological weapons are living, disease-causing agents developed and cultivated to be used as weapons of war. Both kinds of weapons can be delivered by bombs, warheads, and sprayers.

Historians date the first modern use of chemical weapons in warfare to World War I, during which both sides used chlorine, mustard gas, and other poisonous chemicals (the gas mask was developed during this conflict). Poison gas attacks caused an estimated one hundred thousand deaths and 1.2 million casualties. In 1925, many of the world's nations agreed to the Geneva Protocol, which prohibited the use of poisonous gases and biological agents in warfare. However, despite this accord, several countries, including the United States, Britain, Japan, Germany, and the Soviet Union continued to research, develop, and stockpile chemical and biological weapons. Italy used chemical weapons in Ethiopia, and Japan used both kinds of weapons against China in the 1930s, but the use of these weapons in World War II was for the most part avoided, in part because no country wanted to risk retaliation in kind. President Franklin D. Roosevelt warned the Axis nations that

> Use of such weapons has been outlawed by the general opinion of civilized mankind. This country has not used them, and I hope we never will be compelled to use them. I state categorically that we shall under no circumstances resort to the use of such weapons unless they are first used by our enemies.

A more recent example of a nation that used chemical weapons is Iraq, which deployed chemical weapons against Iran and against Kurdish rebels in the 1980s.

The United States maintained ongoing biological and chemical weapons programs until the late 1960s, when President Richard Nixon ordered a review of them. In 1969 Nixon formally declared that the United States would cease production of chemical weapons and would renounce their use. He went even further with biological weapons, announcing that America renounced biological warfare and would take steps to unilaterally destroy all its stocks of biological weapons (research on defenses against biological weapons would continue). In 1970 the United States extended its ban to cover toxins—poisons produced by biological agents. Nixon also pledged to have the Senate finally ratify the 1925 Geneva Protocol (the Senate voted for ratification in 1975). Some observers noted that the United States had several reasons for forgoing these weapons beyond aversion to their horrific nature and potential for indiscriminate killing. Both chemical and biological weapons are potentially easier to develop than nuclear weapons, placing them within the potential reach of more countries (some have termed chemical and biological weapons the "poor man's atom bomb"). The United States feared that the widespread proliferation of chemical and biological weapons would undermine the military advantage it possessed due to the fact that it was one of the few nations that had nuclear weapons.

In addition to unilaterally curbing its own weapons programs, the United States has worked with other nations to create international antiproliferation treaties against biological and chemical weapons. The Biological and Toxin Weapons Convention (BTWC) was negotiated under the auspices of the United Nations in 1972 and entered into force in 1975; its signatory nations agreed to ban the development, testing, and storage of such weapons. By 2000 more than 160 nations had signed the treaty. The Chemical Weapons Convention (CWC) was negotiated and signed in 1993 and entered into force in 1997. Its 174 signatory nations (as of 2000) pledged to either not build chemical weapons or to destroy their existing stocks within ten to fifteen years. The chemical weapons treaty, unlike the BTWC, includes mechanisms for verifying compliance. The United States has signed and ratified both treaties.

Some people have questioned the ultimate effectiveness of these international treaties. Some nations suspected of possessing chemical weapons—such as Egypt, Syria, and Israel—have declined to sign on to the Chemical Weapons Convention. In addition to concerns about nations who have not signed or are cheating international treaties, many worry that international bans have no effect on terrorist groups. In recent years both types of weapons have been used in acts of terrorism. The religious cult Aum Shinrikyo used sarin gas, a nerve agent, in a 1995 attack in a Japanese subway station that killed twelve and wounded thousands. Documents found in Afghanistan in 2001 found that the al Qaeda terrorist network had supported research on developing biological and chemical weapons. Also in 2001, letters containing anthrax—a toxin created by the species of bacteria—were mailed to members of Congress and other individuals. The cases caused significant social disruption and panic in some areas and highlighted the continuing anxiety caused by such weapons in the United States.

Examining Cartoon 1:
"The Gas Fiend"

About the Cartoon

The modern history of weapons of mass destruction began in April 1915 during World War I, when the German army released chlorine gas from cylinders, causing a greenish yellow cloud to roll across the battlefield and kill or injure twenty-eight hundred soldiers. It was the first strategic use of a chemical weapon to inflict mass casualties. Great Britain soon retaliated with similar attacks; 124,000 tons of chemical weapons were used by all sides before World War I ended in 1918. In 1925 world leaders signed the Geneva Protocol prohibiting the use of chemical weapons.

The anti-Germany cartoon here depicts one of these first chemical weapons attacks. It shows a sleeping soldier in a trench, soon to be enveloped in gas released by an ominous-looking serpent.

About the Cartoonist

Louis Raemaekers was a Dutch political cartoonist who became famous in World War I for his critical cartoons of Germany. His work was widely seen not only in Holland, but also Great Britain and the United States. His cartoons were later collected in *Raemaekers Cartoon History of the War*, published in 1919.

Raemaekers. *The Great War, a Neutral's Indictment: One Hundred Cartoons*. London: Fine Art Society, 1916.

Examining Cartoon 2

About the Cartoon

The 1925 Geneva Convention prohibited use of chemical weapons but did not prohibit developing and stockpiling them. Negotiations to create a new treaty banning chemical weapons began in the 1980s; in 1993, shortly before he left office, President George H.W. Bush signed the Chemical Weapons Convention (CWC), a treaty that prohibits the development, production, and stockpiling of chemical weapons. However, the U.S. Senate refused to ratify the treaty for several years. In early 1997 President Bill Clinton again submitted the CWC to the Senate for ratification. Senator Jesse Helms of North Carolina, then the Republican chair of the Senate Foreign Relations Committee, led the opposition to the treaty, maintaining it was unenforceable and ineffective. The above cartoon shows Clinton in a protective suit carefully disarming a chemical weapons bomb, at the heart of which lies the face of Helms. Clinton must "defuse" Helms's resistance to signing the treaty in order to place it in effect and thereby disarm the bomb that represents chemical weapons arsenals in America and the world. Despite Helms's opposition, the U.S. Senate voted 74-26 on April 24, 1997, in favor of ratification, making the United States the eighty-eighth nation in the world to ratify the treaty.

About the Cartoonist

Dwane Powell is a longtime editorial cartoonist of the *Raleigh News & Observer*.

Examining Cartoon 3:
"A Higher State of Alertness"

About the Cartoon

For many Americans, the threat of chemical and biological weapons hit close to home in the fall of 2001 when a series of letters containing a white powder form of anthrax were mailed to political and media figures. Anthrax is a disease caused by a kind of bacteria that exists in livestock animals; "weaponizing" anthrax into a powder form has been a central focus of biological weapons research by many countries. The letters scare, coupled with the September 11, 2001, terrorist attacks involving hijacked jetliners, created a heightened sense of nervousness among Americans. Many rushed to buy gas masks and the antibiotic Cipro (used to treat anthrax) as precautions. This state of affairs is illustrated in this cartoon. John Ashcroft, the nation's attorney general, appears on the television to tell Americans to be aware of possible terrorist attacks involving chemicals or anthrax—but the person in a protective suit near a box of Cipro appears to be as "alert" as can be.

About the Cartoonist

Jack Ohman is political cartoonist of the *Oregonian;* his work is also nationally syndicated.

Chapter 4

Iraq's WMDs—
Danger or Hype?

EXAMINING ISSUES THROUGH
POLITICAL CARTOONS

Preface

A recent controversial historical event in which weapons of mass destruction played a central role was the 2003 Iraq War. Iraq had long been under international scrutiny about its weapons of mass destruction (WMDs) and for years had been under economic sanctions imposed by the United Nations (UN). President George W. Bush's decision to lead a coalition of nations to invade and occupy Iraq was based on his judgment that international sanctions were not working and that Iraq under its leader Saddam Hussein possessed chemical, biological, and possibly even nuclear weapons in defiance of UN resolutions. The controversy over Bush's 2003 decision increased when inspectors failed to find any WMDs once American and allied troops deposed Hussein and occupied Iraq by May 2003.

No one disputed the fact that Iraq had a long and dubious history of developing and even using WMDs. Indeed, Iraq can be considered a useful case study in comparing different approaches to preventing the proliferation of WMDs. Iraq started developing a nuclear program around 1970, although as a signatory nation of the Nuclear Nonproliferation Treaty (NPT), it had to keep its efforts secret. A nuclear power reactor that could produce weapons-grade plutonium was bombed by Israel in 1981. Iraq also began both biological and chemical weapons programs in the 1970s; among the agents it developed were the nerve agents sarin and VX; mustard gases; and ricin, anthrax, and other toxins and biological agents. These actions were also taken in defiance of international treaties, including the 1972 Biological and Toxin Weapons Convention (BTWC). Iraq used chemical weapons in its 1980–1988 war against Iran, as well as against Kurdish insurgents in 1988.

The full extent of Iraq's WMD programs became clearer to the outside world following the 1991 Persian Gulf War, in which Iraq's attempt to occupy its neighbor Kuwait resulted in defeat by a UN coalition of nations. As part of its surrender, Iraq agreed to account for and destroy all of its WMDs, and UN inspectors thus gained unprecedented access to Iraq's WMD programs. From 1991 to 1998 international inspectors located and destroyed a vast undeclared arsenal of WMDs, including 690 tons of chemical weapons agents and thousands of tons of precursor chemicals at a biological weapons facility. In 1998 Saddam Hussein expelled all UN inspectors, leaving Iraq under a state of economic sanctions first imposed in 1991. With inspectors gone, the state of Iraq's WMD programs became uncertain to the outside world. This uncertainty remained even after President Bill Clinton ordered bombing strikes against suspected Iraqi WMD facilities in late 1998.

International inspectors returned in late 2002 after the United Nations, at the urging of President George W. Bush, passed a new resolution calling on Iraq to demonstrate proof of WMD disarmament or face "serious consequences." In February 2003, chief UN inspector Hans Blix reported that while no actual weapons of mass destruction had been found, Hussein still was not fully cooperating with the international observers. Some argued that the approach of international inspections and economic sanctions was indeed working and that Iraq's WMD threat had been contained if not eliminated. Others, including President Bush, argued that UN-led efforts to disarm Iraq were not working and that more direct military action was called for. In his speech to the nation on the eve of military action in 2003, Bush justified his decision primarily on the grounds that Iraq possessed WMDs, including chemical and biological weapons, and was seeking nuclear weapons as well—all in defiance of UN resolutions: "Intelligence gathered by this and other governments leaves no doubt that the Iraqi regime continues to possess and conceal some of the most lethal weapons ever devised."

While differences of opinion existed as to the extent of Iraq's WMD programs, most experts believed that Iraq harbored at least some weapon stockpiles. However, since Bush's decision, no WMDs have been found in Iraq. Following Hussein's ouster, David Kay was tapped by President Bush to head the Iraq Survey Group, a team of fourteen hundred people sent to find Iraq's WMDs. After seven months of work, interviews with thousands of Iraqis, and research through millions of documents, no WMDs were found. Kay resigned from the Iraq Survey Group in January 2004; in February he testified before the Senate that "we were almost all wrong" in assumptions about Iraq and that "it is highly unlikely that there were large stockpiles of deployed militarized chemical and biological weapons there." The failure to find WMDs in Iraq has raised doubts about Bush's decision to go to war and the intelligence he was provided with to reach that decision. Whether the Iraq war provides a model for the United States in dealing with other suspect nations, such as Iran and North Korea, remains an open question.

Examining Cartoon 1:
"We Don't Get It"

About the Cartoon

The United States invaded Iraq in March 2003. President George W. Bush had been laying diplomatic groundwork for the invasion for months prior to that. The above cartoon depicts Bush's key arguments for war, including the charge that Iraqi leader Saddam Hussein was developing chemical, biological, and nuclear weapons of mass destruction and could eventually supply such weapons to terrorist groups that opposed the United States. Bush's campaign on the necessity of "regime change" in Iraq was met with skepticism and resistance by leaders of other nations. This cartoon depicts Bush as a frustrated teacher of children who, despite his best efforts, fail to grasp his points. The students represent other nations; one student is wearing a French beret, for example, while another is wearing the traditional head covering of Saudi Arabia. The cartoonist is criticizing other nations by depicting them as children who are unable to understand the obvious facts.

About the Cartoonist
Gary Varvel has been the editorial cartoonist for the *Indianapolis Star* since 1994.

Examining Cartoon 2:
"Thank You for Coming"

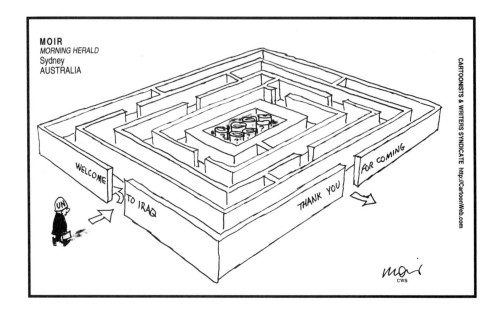

About the Cartoon

Following Iraq's defeat in the 1991 Persian Gulf War, the nation's leader, Saddam Hussein, agreed to relinquish all of Iraq's weapons of mass destruction. From 1991 to 1998 UN weapons inspectors made periodic trips to Iraq and were able to uncover some evidence of a nuclear weapons program and to find and destroy chemical and biological weapons. Many observers suspected Hussein was successfully keeping some weapons hidden—a suspicion that grew when Hussein expelled UN weapons inspectors in 1998. UN inspectors returned in late 2002 after the United Nations, at the urging of U.S. president George W. Bush, passed a new resolution calling for Iraq to demonstrate proof of disarmament or face "serious consequences." But many doubted whether these new teams of inspectors would be able to find weapons Hussein wished to hide. This cartoon by the Australian cartoonist Alan Moir depicts the presumed futility of relying on the United Nations to find Iraq's suspected weapons of mass destruction. The cartoon shows a UN inspector entering Iraq, which is represented as a maze in which none of the paths leads to the stash of chemical weapons in the middle. The United States, arguing that the United Nations had failed to demonstrate Iraq's weapons-free status, invaded and occupied that nation in March 2003.

About the Cartoonist

Alan Moir, one of Austrialia's leading political cartoonists, has worked for the *Sydney Morning Herald* since 1984.

Examining Cartoon 3:
"Get Them Faster?"

About the Cartoon

The above cartoon was published shortly before the United States led a multinational coalition against Iraq in 2003. This act was justified as a necessary measure to prevent Iraq's leader Saddam Hussein from using chemical, nuclear, or biological weapons of mass destruction (WMDs) against the United States or from supplying such weapons to terrorists who might use them to attack America. Iraq had denied possessing weapons of mass destruction, but had not cooperated fully with international arms inspectors from the

United Nations nor proven to America's satisfaction that it had no WMDs. However, at the same time the United States was calling for military action against Iraq, it was pursuing multilateral diplomatic talks with North Korea, a country that had repudiated arms control agreements, expelled international arms inspectors, and openly claimed it had nuclear bombs in its possession. Some observers argue the fact that North Korea already was believed to possess nuclear weapons deterred the United States from pursuing military action there.

This cartoon, like the one by Gary Varvel, shows President George W. Bush as a teacher to the world. The lesson Bush presumably wants to teach is that other nations should refrain from developing any WMDs if they want to avoid military consequences from the United States. But the response from one of the "students" suggests that Bush's teaching efforts may have the opposite effect. Nations might conclude that the way to avoid military attack from the United States is to emulate North Korea, not Iraq, and successfully develop such weapons.

About the Cartoonist

Tom Toles, an editorial cartoonist for the *Washington Post* and former cartoonist for the *Buffalo News*, won the 1990 Pulitzer Prize for political cartoons.

Examining Cartoon 4:

"Weapons of Mass Deception"

WMD EXCUSE FOR INVADING IRAQ

Ottawa Citizen
Caglecartoons.com

WEAPON OF MASS DECEPTION

About the Cartoon

The possibility that Iraq was developing and stockpiling weapons of mass destruction (WMDs) was cited as a primary justification in the decision by President George W. Bush to lead a coalition of nations to invade and occupy Iraq in 2003. After the U.S.-led coalition toppled the regime of Saddam Hussein, Bush sent in the Iraq Survey Group, a team of inspectors led by diplomat David Kay, to find and secure Iraq's weapons and facilities. But months of searching failed to uncover any evidence of WMDs. In January 2004 Kay resigned his post and testified before a Senate hearing that no such weapons were to be found in Iraq and that America's prewar intelligence on Iraq's WMDs was probably "all wrong."

Some critics of the Bush administration argue that wrong predictions regarding Iraq's WMDs stem from more than intelligence failures. They accuse the Bush administration and the president himself of hyping and overstating the intelligence they had to convince the American people to support war in Iraq. Some have gone so far as to accuse the president of deliberately lying. This accusation is made in visual form in this cartoon. The cartoon alludes to the familiar children's story of Pinocchio, the wooden puppet whose nose would grow when he told a lie.

About the Cartoonist

Cam Cardow is editorial cartoonist for the *Ottowa Citizen*. His work has appeared in most of Canada's leading newspapers as well as the *New York Times* and *USA Today*.

Chronology

1899
Two dozen nations sign the Hague Convention pledging not to use toxic gases or other poisons as weapons.

1905
The physicist Albert Einstein publishes his theory that matter is a form of energy and that mass and energy are related by the equation $E=mc^2$.

1914–1918
Chemical weapons are used, beginning with Germany's chlorine gas attack in April 1915. The gas causes 1.3 million injuries and one hundred thousand fatalities by the war's end.

1918
The United States establishes the Chemical Weapons Service, its first formal chemical weapons program.

1925
The Geneva Protocol bans the use of chemical and biological weapons in war; the treaty is not ratified by United States and is not signed by Japan.

1932–1945
Japan kills an estimated 260,000 people in China with the plague germ and other biological weapons.

1935
Italy uses mustard gas in its conquest of Abyssinia (Ethiopia).

1939

Albert Einstein signs a letter drafted by physicist Leo Szilard to President Franklin D. Roosevelt telling him that an atomic bomb is feasible.

1941

In December President Franklin D. Roosevelt commits the U.S. government to building an atomic bomb; the secret undertaking becomes known as the Manhattan Project.

1942

A group of Manhattan Project scientists at the University of Chicago produce the world's first artificially created nuclear chain reaction.

1945

The United States explodes the first atomic bomb in New Mexico. It drops an atomic bomb on Hiroshima on August 6 and on Nagasaki on August 9.

1946

The United States proposes that all nuclear materials and technology be placed under international control; the plan is rejected by the Soviet Union.

1949

The Soviet Union successfully tests an atomic bomb, ending America's nuclear monopoly.

1952

The United States explodes the first thermonuclear bomb at a small island in the Pacific Ocean.

Great Britain tests its first fission (atomic) bomb.

1957

Great Britain tests its first thermonuclear bomb. The International Atomic Energy Agency, a UN organization, is founded to help nations develop peaceful nuclear programs and ensure that materials are not diverted for weapons.

1960

France tests its first fission bomb.

1962

In October the Cuban missile crisis brings the world to the brink of nuclear war.

1963

The United States, Great Britain, and the Soviet Union negotiate the Nuclear Test Ban Treaty, in which they agree to not test nuclear weapons in the atmosphere, in outer space, or underwater (underground testing is permitted).

1964

China successfully tests a fission bomb.

1967

China explodes its first thermonuclear bomb.

1968

France conducts its first test of a thermonuclear bomb.

After several years of multilateral negotiations, the Nuclear Nonproliferation Treaty (NPT) is signed by sixty-two countries, including the United States and the Soviet Union.

1969

President Richard Nixon declares a U.S. moratorium on chemical weapons production and biological weapons possession.

1972

The United States, the Soviet Union, and more than one hundred other nations sign the Biological and Toxin Weapons Convention, which bans the possession of such weapons.

The United States and the Soviet Union sign the Anti-Ballistic Missile (ABM) Treaty.

1974

India explodes a small fission device.

The United States and the Soviet Union agree to limit nuclear tests to 150 kilotons.

1979
Sixty-nine people are killed when anthrax spores are accidentally released in the Soviet Union—a development that to some observers confirms the existence of an illegal biological weapons program there.

The United States and the Soviet Union sign the Strategic Arms Limitation Treaty (SALT II) limiting the number of nuclear weapons in the two countries; the treaty is never ratified by the U.S. Senate.

A U.S. satellite detects an apparent South African–Israeli nuclear test off the South African coast.

1981
Israeli jets destroy Iraq's Osirak nuclear research reactor.

1983–1988
Chemical weapons are used by both sides in the Iran-Iraq war, killing thousands.

1984
U.S. president Ronald Reagan calls for an international ban on chemical weapons.

1987
President Ronald Reagan and Soviet leader Mikhail Gorbachev sign the Intermediate-Range Nuclear Forces (INF) Treaty, eliminating an entire class of nuclear-armed missiles.

1988
Iraq, under leader Saddam Hussein, kills five thousand Kurds with mustard gas and other chemicals.

1990
U.S. president George H.W. Bush and Soviet president Mikhail Gorbachev sign a bilateral treaty to halt chemical weapons production and destroy weapons stockpiles.

1991

Iraq, following its defeat in the Persian Gulf War, is ordered by the United Nations to destroy all its weapons of mass destruction and submit to international inspections.

Both the United States and Soviet Union announce major nuclear disarmament initiatives.

1992

The United States announces a moratorium on nuclear tests.

1993

The Convention on the Prohibition of the Development, Production, Stockpiling and Use of Chemical Weapons, also known as the Chemical Weapons Convention, is signed by the United States and other nations; treaty members pledge to destroy their stocks of chemical weapons by 2007.

South Africa acknowledges it had made nuclear bombs, but says all six were dismantled by 1991.

North Korea withdraws from the Nuclear Nonproliferation Treaty.

1994

The United States and North Korea reach a nuclear accord in which North Korea agrees to freeze its nuclear weapons program in exchange for economic aid in building nuclear power reactors.

1995

The apocalyptic cult Aum Shinrikyo releases the nerve agent sarin in the Tokyo subway system; twelve people die and thousands are injured.

1996

All nuclear weapons remaining in the Ukraine, Belarus, and Kazakhstan (all former parts of the Soviet Union) are transferred to Russia.

1997

The U.S. Senate ratifies the Chemical Weapons Convention.

1998

India and Pakistan conduct nuclear bomb tests.

Citing lack of cooperation, the United Nations withdraws its weapons inspectors from Iraq.

2001
Letters containing anthrax spores are sent in the U.S. mail system, infecting twenty-three and killing five.

2002
President George W. Bush singles out Iraq, Iran, and North Korea as part of an "axis of evil" for developing weapons of mass destruction.

The United States withdraws from the 1972 ABM treaty to allow for the development of a missile defense system.

The United States enlists the United Nations to pass a resolution calling for Iraq to disarm or face "serious consequences." Weapons inspectors return to Iraq.

The United States announces that North Korea has admitted to having a secret nuclear weapons program in violation of the 1994 accord. In December North Korea begins to reactivate its Yong-byon nuclear reactor. International inspectors are forced to leave the country.

2003
Citing Iraq's noncompliance with disarmament resolutions, a multi-national force led by the United States invades Iraq. Saddam Hussein's regime collapses in a matter of days. No weapons of mass destruction (WMDs) are used in the fighting.

North Korea says it has finished reprocessing eight thousand nuclear fuel rods, obtaining enough material to make up to six nuclear bombs. It offers to freeze its program in return for American concessions; President George W. Bush says North Korea must first end its program entirely.

The United States and Britain announce the decision of Libya, after nine months of negotiations, to formally dismantle its WMD programs and freeze its nuclear activities. The International Atomic Energy Agency (IAEA) visits four Libyan nuclear sites and assesses that the nuclear program is still years away from being able to produce a bomb.

2004

Abdul Qadeer Khan, the "father" of Pakistan's nuclear weapons program, signs a confession admitting that he provided Iran, North Korea, and Libya with the designs and technology to produce the fuel for nuclear weapons during the last fifteen years.

No WMDs have been found in Iraq. A Senate investigation reports in July that the U.S. intelligence community "mischaracterized" information about Iraq's weapons before the war, but says Bush's administration did not pressure CIA analysts.

New concerns are raised about Iran's nuclear weapons programs after that country submits a report to the IAEA that includes previously omitted details about the country's potential weapons-related research, including designs and components for advanced centrifuges capable of producing weapons-grade uranium.

Organizations to Contact

The editors have compiled the following list of organizations concerned with the issues debated in this book. The descriptions are derived from materials provided by the organizations. All have publications or information available for interested readers. The list was compiled on the date of publication of the present volume; the information provided here may change. Be aware that many organizations take several weeks or longer to respond to inquiries, so allow as much time as possible.

American Enterprise Institute (AEI)
1150 Seventeenth St. NW, Washington, DC 20036
(202) 862-5800 • fax: (202) 862-7177
Web site: www.aei.org

The American Enterprise Institute for Public Policy Research is a scholarly research institute that is dedicated to preserving limited government, private enterprise, and a strong foreign policy and national defense. Articles about weapons of mass destruction and other foreign policy issues can be found in its magazine *American Enterprise* and on its Web site.

Arms Control Association (ACA)
1726 M St. NW, Suite 201, Washington, DC 20036
(202) 463-8270 • fax: (202) 463-8273
e-mail: aca@armscontrol.org • Web site: www.armscontrol.org

The Arms Control Association is a nonprofit organization dedicated to promoting public understanding of and support for effective arms control policies. ACA seeks to increase public appreciation of the need to limit arms, reduce international tensions, and promote world peace. It publishes the monthly magazine *Arms Control Today*.

Brookings Institution
1775 Massachusetts Ave. NW, Washington, DC 20036
(202) 797-6000 • fax: (202) 797-6004
e-mail: brookinfo@brook.edu • Web site: www.brookings.org

The institution, founded in 1927, is a think tank that conducts research and education in foreign policy, economics, government, and the social sciences. Its publications include the quarterly *Brookings Review*, periodic *Policy Briefs*, and books including *Protecting the American Homeland*.

Carnegie Endowment for International Peace
1779 Massachusetts Ave. NW, Washington, DC 20036
(202) 483-7600 • fax: (202) 483-1840
e-mail: info@ceip.org • Web site: www.ceip.org

The Carnegie Endowment for International Peace conducts research on international affairs and U.S. foreign policy. Issues concerning nuclear weapons and proliferation are often discussed in articles published in its quarterly journal *Foreign Policy*.

Center for Nonproliferation Studies
Monterey Institute for International Studies
425 Van Buren St., Monterey, CA 93940
(831) 647-4154 • fax: (831) 647-3519
Web site: http://cns.miis.edu

The center researches all aspects of nonproliferation and works to combat the spread of weapons of mass destruction. The center produces research databases and has multiple reports, papers, speeches, and congressional testimony available online. Its main publication is the *Nonproliferation Review*, which is published three times per year.

Center for Security Policy (CSP)
1920 L St. NW, Suite 210, Washington, DC 20036
(202) 835-9077 • fax: (202) 835-9066
e-mail: info@centerforsecuritypolicy.org
Web site: www.security-policy.org

The center works to stimulate debate about all aspects of security policy, notably those policies bearing on the foreign, defense, economic, financial, and technology interests of the United States. It seeks to promote international peace through American strength. It features numerous articles on the proliferation of weapons of mass destruction on its Web site.

Center for Strategic and International Studies (CSIS)
1800 K St. NW, Suite 400, Washington, DC 20006
(202) 887-0200 • fax: (202) 775-3199
Web site: www.csis.org

The center works to provide world leaders with strategic insights and policy options on current and emerging global issues. It publishes books including *Combating Chemical, Biological, Radiological, and Nuclear Terrorism;* the *Washington Quarterly*, a journal on political, economic, and security issues; and other publications including reports that can be downloaded from its Web site.

Chemical and Biological Arms Control Institute (CBACI)
1747 Pennsylvania Ave. NW, 7th Fl., Washington, DC 20006
(202) 296-3550 • fax: (202) 296-3574
e-mail: cbaci@cbaci.org • Web site: www.cbaci.org

CBACI is a nonprofit corporation that promotes arms control and nonproliferation, with particular focus on the elimination of chemical and biological weapons. It fosters this goal by drawing on an extensive international network to provide research, analysis, technical support, and education. Among the institute's publications is the bimonthly report *Dispatch* and the reports "Bioterrorism in the United States: Threat, Preparedness, and Response" and "Contagion and Conflict: Health as a Global Security Challenge."

Federation of American Scientists Chemical and Biological Arms Control Program
1717 K St. NW, Washington, DC 20036
(202) 546-3300 • fax: (202) 675-1010
e-mail: fas@fas.org • Web site: www.fas.org

The Federation of American Scientists is a privately funded, non-profit organization engaged in analysis and advocacy on science, technology, and public policy for global security. Its Chemical and Biological Arms Control Program works to prevent the development and use of biological weapons. The federation requests that students and other researchers first investigate the resources available on its Web site, such as the paper *Biological Weapons and "Bioterrorism" in the First Years of the 21st Century*, before requesting further information.

Henry L. Stimson Center
11 Dupont Circle NW, 9th Fl., Washington, DC 20036
(202) 223-5956 • fax: (202) 238-9604
Web site: www.stimson.org

The Stimson Center is an independent, nonprofit public policy institute committed to finding and promoting innovative solutions to the security challenges confronting the United States and other nations. The center directs the Chemical and Biological Weapons Nonproliferation Project, which serves as a clearinghouse of information related to the monitoring and implementation of international treaties regulating weapons of mass destruction. The center produces occasional papers, reports, handbooks, and books on chemical and biological weapon policy, nuclear policy, and eliminating weapons of mass destruction.

Union of Concerned Scientists (UCS)
2 Brattle Sq., Cambridge, MA 02238
(617) 547-5552 • fax: (617) 864-9405
e-mail: ucs@ucsusa.org • Web site: www.ucsusa.org

UCS is concerned about the impact of advanced technology on society. It supports nuclear arms control as a means to reduce nuclear weapons. Its publications include the quarterly *Nucleus* newsletter and reports and briefs concerning nuclear proliferation.

United States Arms Control and Disarmament Agency (ACDA)
320 Twenty-first St. NW, Washington, DC 20451
(800) 581-ACDA • fax: (202) 647-6928
Web site: www.acda.gov

The mission of the agency is to strengthen the national security of the United States by formulating, advocating, negotiating, implementing, and verifying effective arms control, nonproliferation, and disarmament policies, strategies, and agreements. In so doing, ACDA ensures that arms control is fully integrated into the development and conduct of U.S. national security policy. The agency publishes fact sheets on the disarmament of weapons of mass destruction as well as online records of speeches, treaties, and reports related to arms control.

For Further Research

Books

Ken Alibek with Stephen Handelman, *Biohazard: The Chilling True Story of the Largest Covert Biological Weapons Program in the World—Told from Inside by the Man Who Ran It*. New York: Random House, 1999.

Graham T. Allison, *Avoiding Nuclear Anarchy: Containing the Threat of Loose Russian Nuclear Weapons and Fissile Material*. Cambridge, MA: MIT Press, 1996.

Wendy Barnaby, *The Plague Makers: The Secret World of Biological Warfare*. New York: Continuum, 1999.

Paul S. Boyer, *Fallout: A Historian Reflects on America's Half-Century Encounter with Nuclear Weapons*. Columbus: Ohio State University Press, 1998.

British Medical Association, *Biotechnology, Weapons, and Humanity*. Amsterdam: Harwood Academic, 1999.

Richard Butler and James C. Roy, *The Greatest Threat: Iraq, Weapons of Mass Destruction, and the Crisis of Global Security*. New York: Public Affairs, 2001.

Joseph Cirincione et al., *Deadly Arsenals: Tracking Weapons of Mass Destruction*. Washington, DC: Carnegie Endowment for International Peace, 2002.

Leonard A. Cole, *The Eleventh Plague: The Politics of Biological and Chemical Warfare*. New York: W.H. Freeman, 1997.

74

Eric Croddy et al., *Chemical and Biological Warfare: A Comprehensive Guide for the Concerned Citizen*. New York: Copernicus Books, 2002.

Malcolm Dando, *Preventing Biological Warfare: The Failure of American Leadership*. New York: Palgrave Macmillan, 2002.

Stephen L. Endicott, *The United States and Biological Warfare: Secrets from the Early Cold War and Korea*. Bloomington: Indiana University Press, 1998.

Robert H. Ferrell, ed., *Harry S. Truman and the Bomb: A Documentary History*. Worland, NY: High Plains, 1996.

John Lewis Gaddis et al., eds., *Cold War Statesmen Confront the Bomb: Nuclear Diplomacy Since 1945*. New York: Oxford University Press, 1999.

Jeanne Guillemin, *Anthrax: The Investigation of a Deadly Outbreak*. Berkeley: University of California Press, 2001.

Khidhir Hamza with Jeff Stein, *Saddam's Bombmaker: The Terrifying Inside Story of the Iraqi Nuclear and Biological Weapons Agenda*. New York: Scribner, 2000.

Sheldon H. Harris, *Factories of Death: Japanese Biological Warfare, 1932–1945, and the American Cover-Up*. New York: Routledge, 1994.

Robert Hutchinson, *Weapons of Mass Destruction: The No-Nonsense Guide to Nuclear, Chemical and Biological Weapons Today*. London: Weidenfeld & Nicolson, 2003.

Stuart E. Johnson, ed., *The Niche Threat: Deterring the Use of Chemical and Biological Weapons*. Washington, DC: National Defense University Press, 1997.

Michael Klare, *Rogue States and Nuclear Outlaws*. New York: Hill and Wang, 1995.

R. Everett Langford, *Introduction to Weapons of Mass Destruction: Radiological, Chemical, and Biological*. New York: John Wiley & Sons, 2004.

Herbert M. Levine, *Chemical & Biological Weapons in Our Times*. New York: Franklin Watts, 2000.

Norman Mailer, *Why Are We at War?* New York: Random House, 2003.

Tom Mangold and Jeff Goldberg, *Plague Wars: A True Story of Biological Warfare*. New York: St. Martin's Press, 2000.

Judith Miller, Stephen Engelberg, and William J. Broad, *Germs: Biological Weapons and America's Secret War*. New York: Simon & Schuster, 2001.

Janne E. Nolan et al., *Ultimate Security: Combating Weapons of Mass Destruction*. New York: Century Foundation Press, 2004.

Keith B. Payne, *Deterrence in the Second Nuclear Age*. Lexington: University Press of Kentucky, 1996.

Kenneth M. Pollack, *The Threatening Storm: The Case for Invading Iraq*. New York: Random House, 2002.

Thomas Powers, *Heisenberg's War: The Secret History of the German Bomb*. New York: Knopf, 1993.

Richard Preston, *The Demon in the Freezer*. New York: Random House, 2002.

Ed Regis, *The Biology of Doom: The History of America's Secret Germ Warfare Project*. New York: Henry Holt, 1999.

Richard Rhodes, *The Making of the Atomic Bomb*. New York: Simon & Schuster, 1986.

Scott D. Sagan and Kenneth N. Waltz, eds., *The Spread of Nuclear Weapons: A Debate*. New York: W.W. Norton, 1995.

Jonathan Schell, *The Unfinished Twentieth Century: The Crisis of Weapons of Mass Destruction*. New York: Verso, 2003.

Scientific American, ed., *Understanding Germ Warfare*. New York: Warner Books, 2002.

Micah L. Sifry and Christopher Cerf, eds., *The Iraq War Reader: History, Documents, Opinions*. New York: Touchstone Books, 2003.

Jessica Stern, *The Ultimate Terrorists*. Cambridge, MA: Harvard University Press, 2001.

Ronald Takaki, *Hiroshima: Why America Dropped the Atomic Bomb*. Boston: Little, Brown, 1995.

Tim Trevan, *Saddam's Secrets: The Hunt for Iraq's Hidden Weapons*. North Pomfret, VT: Trafalgar Square, 1999.

Jonathan B. Tucker, ed., *Toxic Terror: Assessing Terrorist Use of Chemical and Biological Weapons*. Cambridge, MA: MIT Press, 2000.

Allan M. Winkler, *Life Under a Cloud: American Anxiety About the Atom*. New York: Oxford University Press, 1993.

Raymond A. Zilinskas, ed., *Biological Warfare: Modern Offense and Defense*. Boulder, CO: Lynne Rienner, 1999.

Index

Gorbachev, Mikhail, 26, 34

Helms, Jesse, 46–47
Herblock. *See* Block, Herbert L.
Hiroshima (Japan), 6–8, 16, 19, 21
Hussein, Saddam, 52, 56–57, 58
hydrogen bomb, 25

India, nuclear testing by, 36
intercontinental ballistic missiles (ICBMs), 25
Iraq Survey Group, 60–61
Iraq War (2003), 51
    justification for, 54–55
        was based on false intelligence, 52, 60–61
Italy, use of chemical weapons by, 41

Japan
    atomic bombing of, 6–7, 16, 19, 21
    use of chemical/biological weapons by, 41

Kay, David, 52, 53, 60, 61

Laqueur, Walter, 12
London Evening Standard (newspaper), 20
Low, David, 20, 21

Manhattan Project, 15
Moir, Alan, 56, 57
mustard gas, 8
mutually assured destruction (MAD), 25

Nagasaki (Japan), 6–7, 16, 19, 20
nerve agents, 8
New York Sun (newspaper), 29
Nixon, Richard, 42
North Korea
    development of nuclear weapons by, 38–39
    vs. Iraq, U.S. response to, 59
Nuclear Nonproliferation Treaty (1968), 11, 38, 51
nuclear testing, 10–11
nuclear weapons, 6
    effects of, 7–8
    spread of, 26–27
    types of, 7
    U.S.-Russian agreement to deactivate arsenals of, 35
    see also hydrogen bomb

Ohman, Jack, 48, 49
Ottowa Citizen (newspaper), 61

Pakistan, nuclear testing by, 36
Persian Gulf War (1991), 52, 56
Potsdam Conference (1945), 15
Powell, Dwane, 47
Putin, Vladimir, 35

al Qaeda, 43

Raemaekers, Louis, 44, 45
Reagan, Ronald, 35
Richmond Times-Dispatch (newspaper), 19

Roosevelt, Franklin D., 41